Allegro To Life

Earl Vincent de Berge

ISBN: 978-81-8253-850-4

First Edition: 2022
Rs. 200/-

Cyberwit.net
HIG 45 Kaushambi Kunj, Kalindipuram
Allahabad - 211011 (U.P.) India
http://www.cyberwit.net
Tel: +(91) 9415091004
E-mail: info@cyberwit.net

Printed at Thomson Press India Limited.

FOREWORD AND ACKNOWLEDGEMENTS

From 1959 when I wrote my first poem to today, my world view has evolved as I, as do we all, try to grasp the impact of humanity as it buoys or extinguishes individuals and our spaceship planet Earth. I date and identify where I wrote some of my poems to provide readers with points of reference. My approach to poetry is ever evolving but two central principle still guide me: less is almost always more, and, I try to use words and grammar my west Texas mother could understand. Li Po is my hero.

I enjoy describing events and beautiful things in nature and people. The Sonoran deserts of Mexico and Arizona and the people of Guatemala are of special interest to me. Equally pleasureful is doing my level best to skin mean or greedy politicians, business moguls and religious hucksters. This traces to my training as a political scientist and decades of doing voter and market research for politicians and mega corporations. Seen from the inside, things are often worse even than I thought.

I write of what I see, hear, read and dream. My basic focus is that of a naturalist, center-left observer willing to cast neutrality into its sterile corner. After all, our planet and civilizations are on fire with avarice, poverty and despoilments, all fed by would-be dictators, greed-saturated moguls and corporations, and by rigid religious dogma. I try not to sink into cynical despair but rather, to encourage all generations to be hopeful, creative, aware and willing to push back against dogma and greed, whether it comes from business, religious or political bloviators.

Several individuals and entities have been important in encouraging me to write prose, essays and poetry. They include Mark Winheld, P.J. Erickson, Russell Avery, Suzanne, my bride of six decades, Cynthia Hogue, Terrance Bracy, John Gabusi, Jim Haynes, Diane Christensen,

Linda de Berge Firestone, Steve Tuttle, and Antioch College where I learned that if people can't fathom the meaning of my words, as I mean them, it is my fault.

And special thanks to Dr. Karunesh Kumar Agrawal at Taj Mahal Review for taking an interest in my poetical efforts and producing this book.

Earl Vincent de Berge 2021

Contents

"Songs from My Life"

POETRY BEGINS

The art of poetry begins
in the seam where
the grammar of
communication flowers.

In that seam reality
offers a fresh touch
and a personal view
within the petals of wisdom

RUM SHADOWS

After Ron Boltran shots with friends,
I invite my shadow to accompany me home.
Reluctant, for it is still in a jovial mood
. . . or perhaps, aware I can be careless
when tipsy, it lags behind with the admonition,
"Don't fall, for surely I would disappear".

WONDERFUL ROOM

Some nights when moonlight glazed the desert,
Mark and I found places to sit and smoke
and to chat on music, fine rum and God

or on whether women were gods.
Other times we just listened to nature.
We once imagined the moon sitting at her

vanity slowly powdering her face and then
pursuing the sun through a door on the horizon
into a wonderful room where they dined.

BAY LEAVES

Without so much as a rustle
Bay leaves cascade to the earth,
their crisp shells awaiting millions
of cousins in the chilly atmosphere
of our Fall ambiance.

A second fruition comes as they
spring to life at my passing,
rustling against one another,
crunching beneath my boot
filling the air with festive scents.

Mt Wilson, California 1961

ANCIENT STEVEDORE

Quiescent atop coiled hawsers
on the La Paz ship loading dock,
a thin old stevedore finishes his tortilla.

Still strong, but tired, his gnarled hands
lie inert, palms up across his bony lap,
both dusted white from flour bags.

A thick white mustache and eyebrows
on sun blackened patriarchal face ennoble
a gent who ought be pridefully retired

and bouncing grandchildren, or sneaking sips
of rum now and then amidst checkers games
with chums beneath palms fronds along the bay.

Too weary even to chat, he gazes unsmiling
with clear jet black eyes into the chasm
of the bay, waiting the foreman's whistle.

La Paz Mexico 1964

SPINNING IN EMPTINESS

Alone in the emptiness of time
spinning toward where we have never
been, we arrive at moments without end
in a time and place not long a home.

Where did time come from ... where is it going?
When is a moment unique to itself,
when the end of every moment is imperceptible
from the dawn and the dusk of the next?

I think, therefore I am.
I cease thinking, therefore I am not.
Clear, simple, all that I need.

The stone eyelid of time blinks at nothing.
I face whatever is next, unafraid and
with my mind focused on perfection
of balance, tolerance and kindness.

Madrid 1978

LOVE IS

Losing one's mind and not
searching to regain it.

Believing that the common
is exquisite.

Finding a new language and
a someone to speak it with.

FOR MY TWO RAYS

A small stand of quaking aspen trees
cluster, white skin naked in winter's breeze,
their golden fall leaves scattered all around.
Bare, up-stretched branches sing no songs
yet their thin fingers seem cupped in prayer –
Oh, winter haze and cold please fade soon,
bring back the warmth of sunlight at noon

For my father and brother who loved these trees

DREAM WORLD

The corridors of my dream world
have countless doors opening into rooms
filled with synapses struggling to connect
thoughts and images received a day, week,
a lifetime ago, but no longer crisp.

Loose ends pop up surrealistically
in black and greys, comically disconnected
or frightening in their connectivity.
Pursuing vaguely familiar paths, my brain
careens through the byways of memory,
peers into alleys and empty closets
that suddenly coalesce in improbable ways,
rearranged worlds teeming with action,
laughter, faces, emancipated yearnings,
flying, and at times, fearsome evil
that I cannot reach in time to arrest.

I have nearly mastered letting curious dreams run,
and can self-awaken from scary ones, half-done.
I observe dreams over my right shoulder;
as might a film producer, but without a script
or voice and anyway, the actors pay no attention.

I write the dream script down upon awakening,
while wondering who hired such strange actors.

A GOOD DAY

Closing the gate
of her modest garden
she gazes back briefly
to remember its health,
the smells of plants and soil.

Eight radishes in her hand,
she crosses the gravel drive,
the gay crunch of stones
sound like an invitation
to the rest of a good day.

FALLING ASLEEP

Cupping your breast in my hand,
your back and soft rump cradled
warmly against me, we lie silent,
except for soft steady breathing,
slowly drifting toward sleep.

Sliding my hand to rest on your hip,
you make a small dove-like sound
anticipating our desire, but with gentle
pressure, I say "lie still, time to dream."

As you slip into slumber's cradle,
I watch kaleidoscopic colors and shapes
on the dark screen of my closed eyes
the strange Rorschach patterns of my light
sensors firing dimly as they retreat toward sleep
.

BLACK HOLES

In dazzling complexities of light,
stars gone supernova begin to
circle in an ever tightening embrace,
a mad dance increasing to breathless
speeds as they collapse into a black hole.

Their violent collapse will warp the
unimaginable immensity of space,
its gravity waves sucking to itself
everything from all horizons
into its dense, timeless yet tiny core.

Black holes are wells of gravity
from which nothing can escape,
not even light., everything vanishes
into perfect, lifeless blackness.

Our old sun star may with time
race elegantly to its own future
as black hole ... leaving us
compressed - undivided
and equal at last.

HIS DREAMS TURNED COBALT BLUE

He built his second wife a desert home
facing the red Papago mountains,
seeing them as inspiration
for love, life and for art.

He looked upon Papago mountains
when the moon was full of promise
and night air warm with romance,
but looking elsewhere, she turned cold,.

His life, he said, became a confusing folly
as the red rocks turned to cobalt blue
amidst lonely bushes on the plain.
and his heart turned hard and bitter.

NEW ORLEANS DIRGE

After buying me a Sumatran cigar
we two shuffle out ebony doors
where, etched in frosted green glass,
graceful long-necked sand hill cranes
stand amidst broad-leaved grasses.

As we tumble into the evening air
the owner leans into the night
to encourage our return for drinks –
we smile, promise, and turn away
anxious to find Cuban music.

Cool air and refreshing mist
greet us -- laden with appetizers,
light pastas hiding morsels
of mushroom, fish and duck
and invisible sauces over crisp
vegetables and very fine wines
fermented by soft-spoken people
in other lands who know their trade,
wines with names only the steward
can pronounce, then, sweet pastries
and slowly sipped cognac.

On the avenue, a younger set
in black and sheer fabrics are
just getting started for the night and
headed for places we will never find.

Strolling the Big Easy's narrow, heaving
sidewalks, my friend casually on my arm,
parting for street lamps posts,
we chat of past amigos now missing,
futures we hope will be sweetly relaxed
and of the latest nuances in politics
while passing all manner of street
immorality, indifference or desire.
Remembering where we are, we laugh
as she shifts her purse to between us.

Then intermittent bold, unearthly fiddler music
commands the night, luring us around corners
like lemmings, to the center of a one-man universe.
He stands as specter in the doorway of a closed
crystal fixture shop, its one security lamp backlighting
him as a large shadow rocking back and forth,
in a billowing grey shirt and black pants.
His music commands the six directions.

His eyes seem fixed on mica flakes
that sparkle like stars in the wet sidewalk.
He saws his bow decisively on the strings
and without pause. Is he improvising
or following a score only he can see?
His music is feverish, the violin varnish
glows with the souls of its maker and player.
Something glitters from his eyes
as enraged 12-tone music cascades
into the narrow streets ... music of Schoenberg
perhaps mixed in his head with intense loathing
of something, perhaps us, well fed, gliding past,
stunned yet pleased at this man's very existence.

As I fish my pocket for money, I think he belongs
in a pugnacious orchestra sick of Wagner's
heroic fantasies and hip hop's puny rhymes,
yet I suddenly feel angry at the improbability
of a man already dead, awaiting coins
while playing his own dirge.

BEFORE ITS TIME

A quarter moon slowly arcs through
oceans of stars burning tiny random holes
in our jet black canopy. Each star a diamond
bringing universal messages audible to those
able to commune with galaxies and suns.

Listen closely, hear the roar
of an expanding universe reduced
by time and distance to vaporous whispers
racing freely in the vacuum of space despite
the restraints of gravity and time.

Galaxies, fiery echoes of their origins,
reveal the unfolding of motiveless energy
spinning into fantastic pinwheels of gravity
racing from massive density to timeless ether
in aimless atomic pulsing lullaby of physics.

Offering no motive for anything's existence
except the laws of physics and the creative forces
of random occurrences within chaos, there comes
an unlikely creation of soft sentient beings capable
of self-change to survive in their environment

But sentient humans breed faster than war, disease, age,
pollution and natural calamities can kill them off.
Thus do humans slowly overwhelm the planet
–fouling land, air and water with billions of their kind
who live in unbridled exploitation, skill and dogma

to over-populate, seek more control, more money and
all at the expense of others and everything
while pridefully pretending "more is better."
The COVID 19 virus and its variants provide lessons:
sciences and technologies can find and muster solutions
but religion and politicians thwart applications and stir fear
until a frightened public divides and turns against itself
and the race to perdition accelerates.

DAWN

Nudged gently,
the dark blue feathers
of night take flight
from a pale downy dawn
growing robust.

Nebraska 1966

HOPI PRAYER

Opening our meeting,
    the Hopi poet offers
a quiet rhythmic prayer.

I do not understand a syllable
    of Hopi,
but his soothing, calming

spirituality fills the room
    and each of us
with positive ruminations.

NATURE'S WOMB

Nature's womb is human destiny
and mankind's future is formed
by the respect we give Nature.

Balancing earth's capacity to provide
against population growth and consumption,
defines quality of life, if not life itself.

The cancerous growth in human numbers
ruptures Earth's fabric with pollution and
depletion that wither Nature's bounty.

Nature has always pushed back with
floods, fire and pestilence, but like ants,
humans just keep breeding and grasping.

Exasperated, Nature now pulls climate
change from her mighty quiver, for Nature
can do what we are loathe to admit - kill us off.

Can we repair our interventions and apply
human ingenuity to visions beyond making
more consumers to increase profits for the few?

WAR, DAY AFTER DAY

Modern war achieves all its goals —
    industrial grade brutality driven by anger and distrust
    killing technologies ever perfected and enhanced
    military budgets sucking civilization dry
    push-button killing, torture, murder of children,
    leveling cities to rubble, pulverizing icons of the ages,
    propaganda to glorify and foster endless hatred.

More to come? Of course!
Mix church and state and profits in war
... Expect the worst.

So called world leaders hustle to make ruin
    of past, present and future,
    of man and community,
they foster hatred among peoples unmet
    while shattering civility at all levels,
    among all men and nations... for generations.

"Mission accomplished" — the words of fools
who mistake "battlefield victory" and revenge, for the end of hatred.
But hatred only breeds more hatred and war's cocktails
of rape, pillage, destruction, genocide, femicide, infanticide,
refugees, disease, starvation, blood on walls, mass graves,
minds warped by what they see and plots for revenge.

day after day
    day after day
        day after day
                day after day ...

DANCE PARTNER

My shadow ponders not whether he is ready
as down a moonlit avenue I stroll to a spot
where we two can dance as friends in purpose.
When I raise an arm – he instantly responds.

Approaching a streetlight's glare
he slides under my feet as if to hide
and when I spin around he is stretched
behind, scratching his head, watching me.

Pressing on past the lamp to escape
his stare, somehow he sprints ahead
with each of my steps, but then fades,
raising a heartfelt fear – have we ceased to exist?.

At the corner beneath four street lamps,
my shadow returns, all at once everywhere
streaking out in different directions and tones,
all on similar, yet different syncopated journeys.

Suddenly a shadow appears but it is stock still
and I am still dancing with my four friends
with twirls and leaps that should impress.
A policeman asks - "You okay mister?"

San Francisco

CARAFE DESIGNS

On a scarred ebony leather
    table top
an empty cut-glass brandy
    carafe stands aflame
catching migrating beams
    of morning sun.

Sunlight refracts and casts
    abstract geometric grey
and blue patterns onto walls,
    windows, ceiling and
onto the blouse and face of my love
    sitting with her book.

The geometry shifts slowly
    in defiance of my desire
for stability of the image,
    yet lingers in the quintessence
of calm and a reflection
    of our peaceful mood.

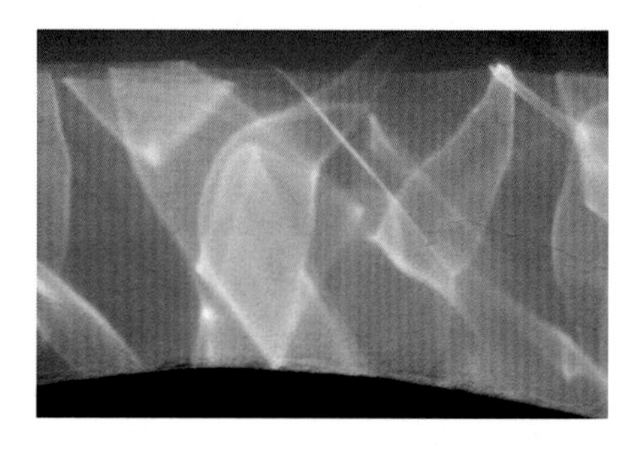

THE OLD SCOUT

Leo rolled down the antiseptic hall
in his wheelchair, until the dining hall
came into view and with it an automatic
glass door to the patio where an aster
flowered bravely in the cold.

He desired to admire and hold it
in his unsteady hand beneath autumn trees
turning from green to gold, red and yellow
along the walkway, where if he could,
he would stroll beyond the red brick walls
of his final home for the old and weak.

Trees waved gaily to him as a modest
wind brushed their tops. For days he had admired
the pink aster beyond the door, tilted slightly
toward him as if in greeting. He knew it might
be the last flower he would ever hold closely
to study and praise, and perhaps honor with a poem.

He tried to push the electric door opener
but lacked the strength, but Victor, a Sudanese
man and patient aide who loved the old man,
saw his desire and opened the door
with the words "Now Leo, it's out cold here,
don't stay too long," then left and returned
almost immediately with a large warm blanket.

Leo sat admiring the aster and debating
with himself whether to pick it for his room.
But he left it alone thinking: "You have only
one season ... I have had 103".

He sat quietly a little closer to nature
and it was a joy: natural things had always
been his friends to think about and admire.

Ladies at lunch tables inside began
to worry about the old man bundled
alone on the patio. They needn't have,
he was warm and happy as a Boy Scout
who had just earned a new badge.

Leo Sonderegger, beloved Father-in-Law and writer

ON THE DEATH OF A MEXICAN BOY

Staring into a scene of death
an emotional flood of fear, anger
and sorrow washed me forever
into an altered world perspective.
There lay a dead boy ...a young boy,
my age perhaps, no more than 13.

Head crushed, chest skinned by
hot asphalt, his blood oozing among
strewn vegetables next to his dad's
old pickup, overturned where it was forced
off the road by an impatient rich bastard
because a "damn Mexican" farmer
was driving too slowly.

Mesa Az

BEAUTIFUL FROM ON HIGH

Lifting in deafening roar and vibration
our Houston-bound aircraft cuts
though clean clear air above green
Guatemala forests and volcanic mountains.

Pilot races to outpace Hurricane Katrina's
massive chaos while between chats
we watch the circling tempest below
thrash Carribean coastlines.

Soon storm surges will cleave levees
in New Orleans, collapse trees on old
French-style homes as poor folk drown
– tho all pray for mercy from their gods.

Katrina's tight concentric clouds seem calm
from above though we know they race each other
in a game of fury to create hell on sea and land.
From here they look like an egg-white meringue.

EDGING AWAY

The moon, so scientists say,
edges away from planet Earth
a foot or so each year,
Be calm, no need for anxiety,
I've plenty of time to bid good-by
for in my 60 years she has fled
only as far as the apricot tree
in my modest front yard.

FIRST IRIS

Spring's first iris emerge
on sensuous stalks, pregnant
with buds swelling to burst into
lavender satin and elegant form.
My pulse quickens, then is at peace
in the sway of such calm perfection.

ENCHANTMENT LOST

Far from pulsing, crowded cities,
night cloaks us thoroughly, offering
enchantment in shrinking rural locales
where one's blood pressure calms beneath
the sea of sparkling stars on the flawless
silken black canvass of a moonless night.

Yet a time creeps up behind us
when none will look up in wonder
to witness the Milky Way's mystifying
broad blanket of stars in an inky sky
punctuated with errant planets rising,
easing west and gently blinking out.

Our night firmaments fade behind
canopies of poison air reflecting
wasted city light. Planet Earth will glow
with light pollution, its starry nights lost.
This cannot be what God meant by
"Let there be light!"

LEFT UNSAID

On sunlit days and moonlit calm
my shadows ever reach back to me,
sliding into my eyes and mind
with wisps of memory bearing
past folly to be contemplated.

Are they calling me to introspect,
perhaps to self-impeach
for deeds still undone —
apologies and encouragements
unsaid to friends who now
or too soon may be dead?

"Poems From Guatemala"

CHIPI-CHIPI

It is raining
in the way of mist,
just heavy enough
to cling to plants
... too light to dimple the lake.

There are no sounds
except sparrows
shrugging their tiny wings
free of water.

Chipi-chipi
is the name
Tzutujil speakers
give to mist rain
that neither
starts nor stops
yet accumulates
like dew
to drip gently from
palm fronds.

One senses eternity.

GREEN ONIONS

Pausing at roadside we watch Maya
women harvesting family plots of green onions.
Sturdy, straight-backed, earth rooted pillars,
they sit upon the ground, their blouses like dabs
of white zinc on the canvas of verdant fields
each elegantly embroidered with Maya icons.

Handloom woven skirts boast traditional designs
on bold swaths of blue, red, and yellow, plus
green, purple and orange, the artistry of sisters,
aunts or themselves, all decorated with animals
and plants that spring from black volcanic soil.

Sun-browned hands move with sureness among
the onions, uprooting and binding into bundles
that women in distant villages will buy.
Each motion releases warm aromatic scents
of green and other onions grown in the valley of Zunil.

On earthen borders separating family plots
youngest sons and daughters scurry happily
with small armfuls to fathers and older brothers.
Each bundle is received with smiles and piled
onto hemp nets, then hefted onto the backs of men –
neck and shoulders taking the weight, each net
spreading like a spider web over the bent men
as they struggle up yet another steep Guatemala hill
as they do for everything that must be moved —
until easing it onto the ground at road side where

overcrowded, growling busses will come anon
to haul bundles and their owners to various markets

My eyes drift back to the harvester women
chatting among themselves, occasionally
bursting into short spells of laughter, enjoying gossip
about some foolish village girl, a wayward husband
or parish priest seduced by his own lust.

When no *chicken bus* is heard on the mountain road,
the valley falls wilderness silent until distant voices
are heard - women singing perhaps at the mission
across the Zunil river or in their yards.
It is an indistinct cacophony of mixed melodies
waxing and waning on gentle breezes wafting
up the valley warms in morning sun.

Intermixed is the rhythm of hands patting tortillas
or the slapping sound of sandals as workers
move about. The smell of onions, water, rich soil
and spiced things cooking somewhere out of sight
teases my brain for local foods we may never taste.

TOUCH

Hand on his arm,
    they circle the park,
decked out in clothing
    of an earlier time
they long for now.

Skin touching gently
    is a private, silent
history book of their lives
    that needs no words.

She squeezes his arm lightly to say
    "look at that child"
he turns without a word to where
    she looks and smiles . . .
his other hand crosses his chest
    to rest upon her fingers
as small words kite up to say
    "Oh doesn't he remind you of ..."
She smiles and looks for others.

The touch of skin known so well,
    happy to be known and loved.
The couple shuffles through their
    remaining space and time,
content in their love.

We watch from a sunny bench,
    Suzanne's shoulder gently against mine.

We know we will soon approach
    their gentle stroll.
I had to age to know why old folks die,
    perhaps too soon
after a mate's passing:
    lonely skin cannot survive
the silence that lingers
    in the lack of touch.
It is an ache that grips the heart
    too hard.

POOR LITTLE HUMMINGBIRD

A rain squall races
across Lake Atitlan
Filling our world with
thunderous liquid sounds.

A hummingbird hides
beneath yucca leaves ...
To her, each drop a
looming bowling ball.

San Lucas Toliman,Lake Atitlan, Guatemala

ESPERANZA WEAVER

Her strong precision hands move
in a centrifuge of ancient time to bring
cultural designs from her marrow into
the fabric on a back-strap loom.

She weaves inside a store's portal
as tourists shuffle past, some stopping
to casually watch and wonder what
her abstract designs might signify.

From her vault of cultural knowledge
does she batten fanciful images with soul?
Do her designs mean something beyond
a weaver's love of nature and hearth?

Silently she sings to her family
in their distant mountain home
around which non-Maya presence is
but a meaningless gust of air.

Loom threads calendar her heart
with images absent the thorns of reality.
The fabric reflects the happiness of
her hands on a loom of gentle dreams.

Xela Guatemala

FORGET ME NOTS

Stepping shyly in front of me,
child-inquisitive, yet driven,
a little Maya girl edges around
my big feet to ask if I would buy
of the trinkets draped on her thin arm.
She, one of twenty children today,
all roses in a land of little.

Missing school, but eager
to help their impoverished families,
each hawks small things to tourists,
begs or explores trash barrels for edibles
discarded by people with much.
They have no time to chase floating
soap bubbles in the park
as do other children.

If only I had not looked into their
forget-me-not eyes and smiles ...
such sweet faces of innocence.
Each child's image nudges me to wonder:
Will they look back on these youthful days
with anger or tenderness?

ABOVE THE MAYAN RUINS OF COPAN

At 65 I place my body and mood
    into a hammock
to rock lazily on a hacienda veranda
    perched high in a hush overlooking
the river valley and Maya ruins of Copan.
    Below, migrating white birds flow
in a soft sunset turning from scarlet
    to brown-gold and blue-grey.

Lazy woodpeckers
    tap slowly on soft wood
in the hazy green distance.
    Breezes rustle big leaves of
tropical trees and dozing comes
    as easily as my quiet
breathing beneath yellow butterflies
    fluttering about the hacienda.

I believe I shall do this again.

CASIMIRA

Civil war widowed Maya mom
just 32, and fond of blue.
Like a fine watch – time proof
in her culture by the lake
where heaven is her cupola.

Her soul, named on grains of rice.
Her youth, once a boundless field,
she dreams of rainbows for her children,
talks to sighing syncretic saints above
the glittering lake, her balcony of dreams.

Holding small secrets behind her teeth
she moves gently, proudly on bare feet
as modern times are pulled like wool
over the eyes of her children and gentle
marimba tones are muted by salsa din.

San Marcos Lake Atitlan. Guatemala

EVER THE VOICE OF SPRING

Antigua mornings after rain –
    ever the voice of spring.
Dew drips from hibiscus,
    hummingbirds thrum,
        fog hues mountains in blue.

Suzanne christened this "the house
    of gentle dreams" in lush gardens,
separate from other lives busy
    in their unfathomable ways.

Beyond the walls marimba music, laughter
    the sounds of children
now and then, a women's
    gentle voice rises and falls
        in solo song.

As the setting sun dissipates the day,
    clouds glow in fine warm golds
as she patio sits reading and listening to
    this ancient town.

Antigua, Guatemala

LEST THEY STARVE

Beneath a canopy of full trees shading
the world of Maya faith, stands a stone shrine
to Pasqual Abaj - staring into the sky
where worshipers know some gods reside.

Thin blue wisps of copal smoke rise
through becalmed mountain air, caressing
pine needles where Sinsontle sings
tirelessly, commanding rain to come.

In humility two women kneel at the shrine
knees and toes on mother earth, as smoke
carries their prayers to end the civil war
to protect their husbands and sons.

No pews nor straight isles lead
to someone exhorting the women
what to believe or to whom to pray
or how to behave when talking to a god.

Their barely audible murmurs ask for
harmony with nature, family safety
and rain for their crops of corn, squash
and beans, lest they all starve to death.

Chichiastenango, Guatemala 1989
Sinsontle: a grey & white mockingbird

GOOD FRIDAY ANTIGUA

I imagine myself hefting the huge *anda* –
leaning into the swirl of blue incense,
my hand, white gloved at my cheek
lifting in lock step with eighty men
the weight of Jesus bearing the cross,
my mind on this day of His passion
— my day of repentance and devotion.

Approaching the central cathedral,
walking over *alfombras* of flowered devotion,
cucuruchos guard our path against
gawking tourists, clicking cameras,
patronizing grins, uncovered heads
and *I love New York* T-shirts.

Incense cleanses the air,
blurs my view of tourist faces
leaning into the veil of incense
as if watching us gives them
understanding of faith.

The crowd fades to silhouettes
— then into nothing
as the rhythm and sway of we eighty
pulls me back into Jesus and his love

IXMUCANE*

The last thing we will give up is hope.
What we will abandon is those last 30 years,
a nightmare that cannot be changed.

The last thing we will give up is hope.
It shows the way to instill children with dreams
of a future they wish to behold and that
reveres the past-future continuum that is Maya.

The last thing we will give up is hope.
With it we share each step toward equality
and can teach the children to forgive our enemies
whose frightened spirits are blinded by hatreds.

The very last thing we will give up is hope
It is the path to rebuild our traditions
And emerge into a fresh world
where hope is far more than a dream.

* personal reflection on "The Granddaughters of Ixmucane - Guatemalan Women Speak" as told to Emilie Smith-Ayala)

A MAN IN CAHABON

After the civil war I met a burly man
in Cahabon, a farm town beyond Lanquin
below the lush valley of Cobán
where orchids festoon the walls.

Barrel-chested, a thoughtful head
adorned with black curly hair
and eyebrows of The Thinker,
his yellow-flowered shirt open
to the sternum; all speak of energy.

A man trusted by his fellows
seeks no advantage, resists any
who would again dangle his people
before the schemes and guns of the rich –
he is a man of his word –
always.

Guatemala, Alta Verapaz

A TEACHER NEAR CHAJUL*

After three decades of civil war
a treaty is signed so armies
might stop murdering one
another and native people.

We rent an old four-by-four
to travel into the remote mountains
of Nebaj and other outposts we had longed
to visit since the music of their names
and history first filled our ears.

On the way, we give a "to-market" ride
to a young Maya mother and then stop
with her for a hillside rest above wild country
to share apples, cheese and crackers.

She gestures down the slope to a roofless
fire-ruined home and whispers "The War" ...
but then looking past that pain,
she speaks brightly of her children … as if
the genocide against her people never happened.

Picnicking in the shadow of a civil war
seems somehow insane but when I ask her about
the future, she chirps happily that the newly paved
road to her village means better teachers
may come to their schools and to her daughters.

The apples taste sweeter.

West of Nebaj in the Ixil Triangle
above Rio Negro, Guatemala

TWO TODDLERS

Two wobbling toddlers explore in plaza mayor —
one wanders from where his Maya mother
sells trinkets to tourists who gloss past
their impoverished lives.

The second, gurgling cheerfully, waddles ahead
of her Ladino father as he follows his angel
toward a life less likely to be so difficult
as for the Maya boy.

Each child chases drifting soap bubbles
launched by vendors hawking their wares.
Iridescent rainbow globes drift
lazily earthward on gentle zephyrs.

Both try to tag a glistening orb,
each swinging chubby little arms
in vain efforts to bat down a globe,
screeching gleefully when one nears.

.

Beneath flowering park trees, their eyes
sparkle with happiness as rainbows
lure them forward with outstretched arms.
Suddenly face-to-face they stop

and topple into each others arms, heads
tipped back, laughing, hugging and
drooling with the unrestrained joy
of rosy expectation.

Like bubbles bursting on the ground, their solidarity
is rudely extinguished as one parent pulls
them apart, unwisely believing that
they cannot, must not, play together.

They may embrace similar dreams,
but will not float in the same currents of life,
and will be segregated in a world
in which they learn to fly ... further apart.

BLIND IN ANTIGUA

Girdled by ancient Spanish buildings,
their silent arches like eyes gazing with
stern conqueror authority into Antigua's
graceful central park where modern folks
now stroll, dally and relax beneath gnarled
jacaranda trees in full lavender flower.

Tropical sunlight pierces the shade to dance
capriciously upon the decompressed shoulders
and smiling faces of visitors and locals as they
watch children dashing around the great fountain
of topless mermaids, their breasts flowing water.

In slow waltz, the calm mix of humanity stir
in social mingling, a seamless stream that eddies,
and pauses on benches where lovers giggle
and women chat in clusters, their hands waving
"oh really!" as they rock back laughing in
the glow of fresh neighborhood chin-wagging.

Travelers praise and bargain with street vendors
selling cashews, Maya fabrics, friendship bracelets,
and "worry dolls" whose miniature baskets are where
people put their worries at night before bedtime.

A man sits with sad slumped shoulders,
one foot raised on the shoeshine boy's box
as he reads of war and butchery in the world.
Worried only about future family meals,

the 11 year old urchin polishes his shoes,
taps the man's toe when the work is done
and opens his small blackened palm
for the few coins he has earned.

Resting on grass in the vogue of nonchalance,
two lads with budding beards and tousled hair
wonder if friends can be made with tourist girls
in scanty summer garb, and in what language.

Shuffling into the park on stiff ankles an old Nun
escorts three black-haired blind children to a favorite
shaded bench near the fountain's splashing waters.
Clad in clean, meager clothing of their small lives,
knees and elbows bare, blue ribbon in the girl's hair,
a cap on each boy and all in open-toe shoes,
they sit quietly and watch the world though sounds
and smells and nature's touch of breezes, warm sun
and the mist of nectar falling from gigantic blossoms
of jacaranda trees above.

Across each face spreads the eloquent countenance
of curiosity ... the images developing in their minds,
unmasked by pretense designed to editorialize.
The celebration of what they see washes unedited
into their smiles, free of guile.

A SENIOR'S LIFE

The old man collects cans at roadside,
every day but Sunday, but not all day.
Longer days would add little to his purse,
or diet nor cure his rock-hard poverty.

At trail's end he flattens the last can,
exchanges yawns with his dog,
rubs his knees and scratches the
mutt's ears before heading home.

Two hours until darkness
as loud speeding hauler trucks
hasten quickly past his shuffle.
He neither scorns nor notices.

Why would he? The poor
are everywhere and he has no
mission but to survive and
not be in anyone's way.

Boca Costa, Guatemala. near Escuintla

CIVIL WAR IN GUATEMALA

Eyes tear at the sight of burned
villages, homes, fields
and accounts of mothers and fathers
vanished in a civil war
that claimed even children
sweet and unaware
in mother's trembling arms.

So many died in the vortex
of surging currents of
a no-mercy war where men with
guns practiced genocide,
hid their foul deeds in mass graves
and earned medals for murdering
men and oxen working plowshares.

Guatemala in this torturous time
is a hideous crucible
where men with guns on both sides
brutalize or stand aside as
citizens are robbed, beaten, terrorized and
murdered wholesale in orgies
of racial and economic inspired genocide.

CARLOS

Each day Carlos awakens - a man in Guatemala.
    Each day he remains a poor old man
shining shoes and snapping his polish cloth
    Pop, swish. Pop, swish. Pop
humming old Maya songs and talking to himself.

I am humble. I have nothing else to be ...
    my village is ruined from the angers of civil war
    and by rich people who swooped in after the killing
    to take every thing from every one ... offering
    nothing except menial jobs.

I used to live in my mountain village
    until the night the army kidnaped me
    and forced me to fight against my people.
    In my nightmares, the chest
    of a humble man like me
    still floats before my gun sight.

When the war ended
    the army threw me away
    and my people turned their backs.

Each evening at mass with my blackened
fingers pressed in prayer, I ask
angels to send forgiveness.

Each morning I remain a poor man
whose name is known to few
but I am calm and no longer live in anger
for God knows what is in my heart.

(Based on conversations with a diminutive soldier/refugee who turned to Antigua after the civil war ended. Carlos died alone in a flop house in 2014)

ALL BUT SHE

For years after the civil war,
when the iron door knocker
shattered the night hush
with its demand, his daughter
went to the door, afraid it would
be a policeman with ghastly news.

But it was always him, unsteady,
drunk, belligerent and complaining
about things she could not decipher
through his slurred words and grunts.

She helps him in, happy he is safe
then weeps again that he remains lost
in a nightmare. She fears that thin
and brain muddled, he will die in an alley
before making peace with God.

All but she have forgotten his misery.

Santo Tomas La Union Guate.

THE CAVE ABOVE CHOCOLA

We hike on a wet black trail
of volcanic ash that bare Maya feet
have pressed into a glistening
path no wider than a human foot
and slick from daily rain.

The path meanders along low reeds
beside a spring fed water ditch,
a rippling treasure making quiet
silver music among the trees and
songs of unfamiliar tropical birds.

Our journey weaves past cattle
pastures and tended corn fields,
none occupied today by shepherds
nor worked by men with hoes.

A woman in native garb carrying
a cloth parcel on her head approaches,
hesitates, then shyly passes,
her bare feet mute on the earth,
her face expressionless.

When past, her pace becomes hurried
as with enigmatic eyes she glances back,
unsure why foreign strangers are on
the trail toward her people's sacred place.
For an instant, her eyes turn dark.

Someone ahead points across the canyon
at an orifice to the Maya underworld
barely visible amidst brush and tall trees,
just a black smudge on the opposite cliff,
a mysterious cave door beside a waterfall.

Leaving the trail we are guided down slope
beside a meadow and past a prized cow tethered
to a mango tree. On the narrow canyon floor,
wild sugar cane and bamboo, boulders
and cascading water make passage difficult.

In the shadow of soaring tropical trees
shafts of sunlight penetrate the shroud
creating dazzling accents on the ground
and on my companion's shoulders
struggling through sub-tropical bramble.

It is a world of damp green moss
and lichen on every surface – trees,
boulders, fallen branches and the earth itself.
Crossing the stream, boots scrape boulders,
leaving marks where bare feet would not.

Past the stream we labor up a wet slope,
through brush slapping at arms and faces,
knocking hats about, boots, knees muddied.
We exchange excited, smiling glances.

The cave looms above, a yawning black hole
the shape of a serpent's open mouth. Sun glaring
on the cliff face makes the cave dark and mysterious.
Waterfall mist creates small rainbows above the cave.

Our troop hesitates, wondering if a shaman
will emerge to shoo us away, but none appears.
The cave is tenderly laid thick with fresh cut flowers.
Candles burn bravely in the darkness and the walls.
are thick with soot from centuries of worship.

Cameras click, two hikers venture inside,
make small observations, point at the rough stone
alter laced with colored stones, feathers, coins
and scraps of paper offered by the pious,
perhaps asking for or giving a blessing.

Helping one another through brush and down
the slippery mud to the stream, our party exits
silently, happy to have seen but to now be away
from a place that belongs to Maya and their jaguars

Chocolá, Guatemala

THANKING GOD FOR CLIMATE CHANGE

Year on year, thanking God for punishing love,
hide-bound farmers cling to failing customs
as creeping climate change unravels
old know-how of what and when to plant.

Longer droughts bake crops, torrential
seasonal rains smash or drown what is left.
Nature's wild seeds find life – double the labor
of planting and growing. Crop yields diminish
and harvest theft becomes a plague.

A pause of gentler weather stimulates planting,
but severe drought follows ... dreams fade as
corn, squash and bean crops wither, family
stores of food shrink and malnutrition becomes
death by starvation among children and elderly.

Women emptied of still-borne babies
rise and work, keeping their hands busy to shield
their minds from tragedies too awful to behold
and from which they can see no escape.

No one hails: *How is your family today?*
In the cold reality of famine, the knowledge
that far too many children and elderly will die
is an anguish too great to share.

Wishing to help, but too weak to hoe, plant
or haul, elders weep in the frightening knowledge,
that they must be left behind, perhaps to die alone
when the able migrate, as poor people always have
to find work and banish their torment with some hope.

Suchitepequez Guatemala

THE PORCH

A man steps onto the empty porch to cry,
caring not - perhaps desiring - that townsfolk,
even strangers, witness his trial.
And we do, including the gas station
attendant and a boy passing afoot.
Both seem sad, yet let it pass,
as if not entirely unusual
in this village overlooking
drought parched crops of maize.

He is a large man, brown skin burning
through a threadbare t-shirt framed by
powerful arms raised to cup his anguished face
as he treads left and right, suffocating in anguish

Loudly his wails rise and fall in
throaty Uspantán, blurred words
we cannot understand ... except that
something has happened to a loved one
or a loved one has committed a treason
to his being or he has committed a treason
against family or friend, or he is simply
exhausted in the struggle to provide.

A woman appears from inside the house,
stands with folded arms and stares at him for
a long moment, then sits down on the stoop.
His wails grow louder as turning, he disappears
slowly into the darkened house.
Looking away, she stares wearily
across the tin roofs below.

Uspantán, Guatemala

CESSPOOL BRAIN

Imagine,
    if you can,
        the cesspool brain
of the Guatemala army colonel
    who ordered the murder
    of hundreds of indigenous
    civilians and their burial
    in his army's latrine pits.

Imagine again
    if you can,
        him walking away,
whistling of a job well done.

Time will fade victim's names
    and the pain of personal loss
but the Maya have not forgotten the
    meaning of their agony.

Genocide is the mother of the next war.

"Desert Songs"

"Mature Boojum tree in the Northern Baja California desert of Mexico"

DESERT AFTER RAIN

Drained ivory clouds drift flat-bottomed
above valleys strewn in yellow froth
where flowering palo verde trees geyser
above cactus spines and creosote brush.

Mockingbird breaks away at my approach,
swoops with intent to distant mesquite.
Unconcerned hummingbirds dart
above, in and out of red ocotillo blossoms.

Drifting in morning air, the scent
of night blooming cactus lingers as
tiny finches make mischief in branches,
then pause to celebrate a day not yet hot.

Nestled near a blueish granite boulder
crimson pin cushion cactus buds open
amid thorns like crowns of fire.
Arroyos are alive with spring life,

Colossal mesquites whisper ancient tales,
fall silent contemplating their love of rain.
All pause before resuming tasks of survival.
A silver dove decants its mournful song.

SEAM OF SILENCE

Lying upon my cot at dawn, eyes lightly closed,
life sounds emerge from desert's vault of silence.

Sleepy birds chirp themselves awake
a creosote bush rustles in a whisper of wind.

Silence returns until a cicada buzzes nearby
then ceases with the abruptness of a slammed door.

Desert eases back into its seam of profound silence
made divine when distant mockingbird launches
her morning aria.

PURSUIT OF SOLITUDE

Aware my pursuit of solitude
    is now an agreeable compulsion,
I find myself standing upon a
    towering ridge looking over
endless folds in silent mountains,
    and unblemished desert,
a remoteness profound and best grasped
    on foot, alone and at risk.

Hills obscure the remote village below,
    but the goat trail ahead forks toward
unknown promises of nature.
    I follow the shunned path
pressing on slowly and pausing,
    to study trifles until
sipping my nearly empty canteen warns —
    neither wanderlust nor curiosity
need lead to suicide by heatstroke.

UNCONCERNED DESERT

My map informs an ocean lies ahead
yet I cannot see or hear it as I tramp
down an arroyo during day's worst heat.

Then, briefly, a stream of cooler air
gifts a whiff of saltiness ... hinting
non-desert lies beyond this cactus scape.

The mountain offers no clue that water
may be nearby and I have come to sense that
desert silence is a disciplined meditation.

This notion settles easily upon me until
I find myself whispering, as if it were a secret,
"nether does the desert care that I am here."

PAUSES HER SONG

A cooing dove pauses her evening song,
looks down nervously as afoot I quietly approach
her night roost high in a young mesquite tree.
Gripping a branch with her tiny red feet
she rises on thin legs, head tilted, eyes
and instincts evaluating if I am a threat.

Uneasy, she lifts both wings, just so,
letting me know she can fly away
or tranquil sit if I just stop looking at her
as might a stalking cat. Her wisdom is
caution, fear ... then flight from those who hunt.
Mine is to look away and let her roost .

SUBTLE GREENS

My mind is calmed by desert's
pastel tan and green colors
capped by a pale blue sky
washed in wispy clouds
off the Pacific, too thin and high for rain.

There is a blanched tonality
to deserts when the sun rides high
as a fiery, unforgiving judge and jury
over what will thrive and what will die.
Incredible ground heat - how do plants survive?

Some see cacti as brutal, even pernicious,
branding them with names like *jumping cactus*
and *prickly pear* whose leaves are sharp spines.
Yet their truth lies beneath waxy skins
where moist elixirs float relaxed and secure.

Imagine cacti as plant sanctuaries
defying the sun's savage rays
and rodents who would devour their skin,
each sanctuary a calm zone
guarding their water ... their life.

I fancy cacti as fortified castles
lush with wild displays of flower and fruit
as nature has had fun with shapes
and splashes of color.

THEREFORE I AM

In Sonoran deserts, long-lived plants are royalty standing patiently in eternal phlegmatic poses awaiting only the gift of rain and insects to nuzzle their flowers. These include the boojum, joshua, tree, yucca, agave, the elephant tree and cacti like the organ pipe, sahuaro and cardon. Although they seem stoically silent, it is a fact known to desert rats that in low telepathic voices cacti debate complex philosophical matters of great meaning to plants. One summer near Arrastras de Arriola while doing very little for several months, I overheard the following exchange:

From an aging sahuaro, who fancies itself something of a planner: *"The logic of plant evolution is not quantitative in nature and depends less upon expenditure, production or investment of energies than upon developing successful strategies for the conservation of the various species and the integration of such strategies into the development of a dominant species.*

After a month of contemplation, a conservative old elephant tree warns in a deep-throated grumble; *"Segregation is the natural order of the species and your dreams of conquest and domination are abhorrent because of their intrinsic and unnatural assumptions of assimilation. Equality in spacing is the central principle in a balanced herbage."*

Down the hill, a young and rebellious Joshua Tree waits barely a fortnight before brashly shouting as loud as his shrill telepathic voice can muster: *"The only effective strategy against the tyranny of plant orthodoxy such as yours, is free criticism amongst and within species, for only in unfettered criticism can we distinguish between our dreams and attainable visions."*

As the three stand quietly meditating on the last utterance, privately thankful things move slowly in the desert and that they are rooted in ground and so cannot engage in fisticuffs, a Cactus Wren sitting atop the old Tory's head proclaims *"I can sing, therefore I am!"* and flies lazily away.

DESERT BUTTERFLIES

Careening from bush to cactus,
all business for nectar.
Zealots in their devotion
to flowers and color,
flitting in zany zig-zag flight,
inattentive to witchery

One careens into a spider web
... too late discovers
attentiveness is key to survival.
The struggle is short,
the spider quick.

There are no successful jesters
in the desert.
No sermons for the deceased.
Life and death go on
No victor says “Thank you.”

HERMIT'S ABODE

Nested at the end of a primitive dirt
road in the Baja outback stands a hermit's
small white-washed adobe home.

Along its west wall, long sprays
of red bougainvillea flowers sway
with each gentle whispering breeze.

Their longest arms twitch as small birds
flitter inside its prickly jungle or dash
away when his old grey dog walks by.

DESERT TORTOISE

Is anyone so alone as a desert tortoise
surviving wilderness at height so low
and pace so appallingly slow?

I've rarely seen one, much less a pair,
so it is a morning treat to watch one
lumbering through camp in slow-mo.

From an ant's perspective — a tortoise
is a domed football stadium moving
ponderously on great leathery legs, crushing
plants, that to the ant are skyscrapers.
Tortoise head and beak-like mouth cast slowly,
from side to side in search of food.
"Not me," pray the ants.

The tortoise's black eyes are calm and unafraid,
the eyes of one who has seen much and
they speak of stoic patience. If threatened, he draws
into his shell, transforming to a stone,
smooth, impenetrable, inert.

His path betrays a single purpose of mind
clambering over small bumps in his path
he moves resolutely straight toward a goal
I cannot see even from my greater height,
but which he must sense ... water, a patch of grass,
a fallen cactus fruit, a lady tortoise perhaps?

Obstructing his campaign lies a large dead cholla,
its Swiss-cheese skeleton in his path,
its dry skin bristling with clusters of spines.
He pauses, surveys the obstacle
and then patiently works his way around,
returning on the far side
to his pursuit of 50 degrees north.

SHAFTS OF LIGHT

Into the humble home, mote-filled bands
of sunlight slip between the yucca stick wall,
silently wafting visual gaiety of clear
light into the somber interior.

Outside, children dart and play,
their shadows now and then blinking
out the golden spotlight circles that
warm the shelves, walls and dirt floor.

The family matron, unable now to lift,
or carry her share of chores watches the
light bring brilliance to forgotten corners
and onto things her hands cared for long ago.

Shoes lying on their sides with tongues,
laces askance ... like her hair. Things
dropped by her children's children,
an antique wooden toy fire truck.

The dusty spotlights are surrogates
for the desert sun above which her
skin and eyes cannot tolerate.

Does she watch the family canary
whose music she may no longer hear
and think of things that please her
or does she listen for angel wings
whispering gently in the golden light?.

Miller's Well, Baja Mexico

THOSE MEN ON THE WALL?

"Those men on the wall?"
The stout old rancher turns slowly
to stare sternly at a wide black and white
photograph in a wooden frame of horses
and men in worn uniforms, saddle kits
and large felt hats. Most had beards.
They were ready to go somewhere,
somewhere serious with rifle and cannon.

"Some say one of every eight Mexicans
was killed in the Revolution. I fought with
those men. That's me near the center.
"Strange," he says pointing vaguely,
"it doesn't seem so long ago,"

A long pause.

"They are all gone now I suppose."
he says turning to stare out the open door
then clears his throat, "Some say one of every
eight Mexicans was killed in the Revolution."

A second long silence.

"My friends are all forgotten now.
No one wrote of where we fought
or who won the dirty battles!
The winners grew fat and had no interest
in the losers and nothing to forfeit by

ignoring this parched corner of Mexico
where the war didn't matter anyway."

With a sneer he adds, "Perhaps I too
would be dead if those bastards
knew how hard I tried to kill them."

Lago Chapala Baja, Mexico

WALLS OF DESENGAÑO

Through Desengaño's ghostly streets
where forfeit dreams drift untold,

winds whisper of bygone times,
of children's voices and guitars.

Wild grasses storm ruined adobe walls.
Alluvium spreads over abandoned byways.

Behind the played-out mining hills
a cooling evening sky pushes gentle air

currents around the melting walls, giving
voice to old conversations that reverberate, die

Desengaño, "Disillusionment" is an abandoned
mining town in northern Baja California, Mexico.

ONLY THE MOON

Rosa stands in the doorway,
half in the shade with only her legs
accepting the sun. Smiling she
watches her old bent husband
cajole and push Maria, their milk
cow, back into the corral
next to their adobe home.

Maria escapes now and again
but never goes far because it is
so darned hot and she knows
that the scent of "after-rain grass"
could be wafting on a breeze
from very far away, where coyote
gangs and mountain lions dwell.

I suppose I might write an amusing
short story about this family of three,
plus their chickens, three Pekin ducks
four milk goats and an old dog,
but it would be so slow-moving
only a full moon would take
time to read it.

CURIOUS SOMBRERO

In a distant desert outback today
I happen upon a curious sight
while tracking a fidgety bevy
of quail, zig-zagging and ever fussing
in the distance, as they so often do.

Wind-blown until snagged
in mesquite branches ten feet
above, rests a straw cowboy hat,
its sunlit brim luffing frail hails
to this passer-by.

Its crown is sun-bleached
to nearly pure white and even its
black silk hat band is faint,
yet the underside of its wakened
brim remains straw yellow.

The sombrero rests owl-like,
surveying the trail below lamenting,
perhaps, that it lacks wings
to magically float down to settle
gently upon my bare head .

FRONTIER GOLD MINER'S CAMP

The gold miner's camp is an 1850 painting.
Towering windmill, blue desert mountains
and clouds frame the tiny settlement.

Five men's quarters cut into an arroyo bank,
are partitioned by flattened cardboard boxes,
shade – palm frond thatch laid on saguaro ribs.

Slow moving donkey pushes a vertical arrastre,
reducing gold-bearing quartz to sand, next to be fed
into rocker and riffled sluice for separation .

Kitchen smoke rises in the still morning air
Rough old prospector sits between his dogs,
rock-hard hands in his lap.

He offers us cups of "cafe de calcetin"
stout steam-brewed coffee filtered
through an old, but clean sock.

,
Yucca and ocotillo corral holds poultry,
another guards maiz and vegetables —
globe mallow dapples the foreground.

Las Arrastras de Arriola -
Baja California del Norte, Mexico 1962 ©

RABBIT IN CAMP

Cotton tail pauses beneath flowering
creosote bush near camp ...
hops cautiously to a cluster
of golden dry seed tufted grass.

I move no muscle that might frighten
the brave little critter. As much as me,
he deserves a tranquil breakfast
nibbling on sweet wild wheat seeds.

He edges closer to where I sit and must
feel safe for he settles on his haunches,
paws uplifted and chews in his bantam way.

When sated, he lies down with ears pressed
close against his body and is just an odd
shaped stone a hawk might overlook.

MOCKINGBIRD'S DELIGHT

Burst open like over-ripe watermelons,
Saguaro fruit beckons to a mockingbird
with ruby-red pulp spangled with shiny black
seeds ripening in mid-morning Sonoran sun.

Haughtily, quickly she lands on the spiny
crown, oblivious to cactus defenses and
now the rich moist fruit is hers alone.
Briefly prisoner to joyous triumph

she begins to voice a blustery song.
But she did not land there merely to brag,
but to fill her belly and enjoy the sweet juice.
Soon she is prying free her breakfast.

Casting aside fruit skin, some seeds fall
to applauding mice below, then lifts her wings
to show her delight for such refreshment, then
cocks her head to check for hawks above.

WHAT TO DO?

Each evening, a middle aged donkey stands alone,
passive on the ranchito's compound boundary
peering into the desert he knows so well.
Sunset paints the desert pastel – so inviting.

Nature smells sweet when the hills turn blue.

Lean and sturdy, the graying gent believes
he could survive on wild grasses and water holes
mapped in his head from so many trips made
each month hauling firewood and things for the family.

What to do? What to do?

He envisions freedom from long trails, belly cinches
and burdens piled upon his back. Freedom from trying days
under the sun when it's too darned hot and he is tired.
"Oh if I could just graze leisurely and bed down

like a deer on a hillside tonight, just over there".

Looking back over the cross he bears, he stares at
the three-room homestead and weighs the certainty
of hauling loads tomorrow - hopefully soft bags of oats.
His owner will cajole him briefly with gentle words
if he rejects slavery by standing defiant, legs locked.

But now he muses, "its not all bad here – carrots,
rub downs, the children, idle hours amid happy chickens
clucking over nothing." Turning, he shuffles into the corral,
before it is locked against predators he often hears at night
and where he can sleep in a peace unfamiliar to deer.

Punta Prieta, Baja Mexico

GOAT HERD DONKEY

The goat shepherd's donkey
is his one-half horse power,
pickup truck, a sure-footed,
trail-tested four-leg-drive critter
with built-in fuel recycling.

Each morning he carries water,
tools and his own fodder, walking
behind the flock. Homeward bound,
his burden is kitchen firewood
and some days, a kid goat that fell ill.

His Eyore face and droopy eyes
suggest a disposition of obedience.
Erect ears imply attentiveness
and long lashes suggest affection —
but he'll kick you if he can!

He knows the drill and does his job
no faster than a switch demands.
He eyes scan the hills where escaped
friends, now feral, roam free of humans
who waste a donkey's precious time!

In the wild one day, he watched
three feral donkeys enjoying grazing
while on a slow paced stroll —
one white, two greys ... none
with lead ropes to curb their will.

Each casually sampling tasty plants along
their trail. Healthy and spry, they kept their
distance from his shepherd master, and cast glares
that said: “Don’t think about a hackamore –
We’re nobody’s slave - not ever again!”

Baja California El Norte

A COYOTE TIPTOES

Picking its wary way, a coyote tiptoes
up the arroyo's steep flank, its skilled
eyes search for a shady spot to digest
the rock squirrel it caught and ate.

Oh you crafty yellow-eyed survivor,
let me enter your arid domain
without disturbing the flow of things.
I'm not a rancher threatening your life.

I glance away for just a moment
and you vanish into nature's realm.
No swirling motes of lingering dust
betray where you have gone.

Adopting your mode beneath this tree
I become irrelevant pretense, like a bush,
never moving a muscle that might warn
... there among cacti, sits a human.

Can I catch sight of you again?
My eyes and brain dissect everything
on your hill for signs you are there,
watching me watching for you.

My wait is long, but finally I see where you
settled down when you lift your head and yawn ...
the two triangles of your ears sign brighter
than a banner in a highway flagman's hand.

Oh Survivor! My admiration for you leaps
the arroyo's swale beneath our pale sky
What see you of me? Immobile, am I here,
or neither a memory nor threat to your safety?

No fear wraps us in this landscape.
We are but curious hunters sitting apart.
A mesquite on the terminus of your hill stands
untroubled by our game of hide and seek.

I GROW CALM

My mind grows calm as
from hillside I see
virgin nature in tranquil pose
with nothing to do but be.

Exquisite desert hush
beneath drifting clouds
that shade shy horned toads and
iridescent tarantula hawks.

Silent limestone canyon walls
and sandy dry arroyo beds
lined with ironwood trees and brush,
all as mute to man as God.

With each year I age, my youthful
ruminations thrust enjoyment
into defense of what man seems
determined to destroy.

Arizona

AN INDISTINCT SOUND

An indistinct sound from the valley beyond
    arrests my mind.
Its unnatural vibration insists on its existence.
    Then silence reclaims the desert.
Rising, I tip my head in search of sounds
    that do not belong – find nothing.

Cicada buzzes briefly — cactus wren responds,
a gentle breeze sniffles, otherwise the desert
lies quiet, indolent, indifferent.

Nearer now, the sounds advances
    in unsteady rumble
through the hills, rises, fades – becomes assertive
    until the battered hulk of a six-wheel
back-country freighter lurches into sight,
    tilting and swaying beneath its canvass top.

Covetous of my solitude and unsure of who they are,
    I stoop in the brush to deny them advantage.
The engine growls in heavy labor and roars when wheels
    lose purchase on loose gravel.
Finally, it lumbers closer, sun on its divided
    windshield glares like orange demon eyes
and its chrome grill seems a mindless frozen grin.

It heaves on the primitive road like a launch
challenging endless waves – slowly crests a hill,
disappears into a ravine, until close below, it passes
through brush, occupants unaware of eyes
watching from the wilderness.

The desert reclaims its tranquility.
White butterflies flutter, each wing a flash of joy.
Ants continue quixotic searches.
Quail dash and plead, doves exchange coos
and cactus wren blusters, "good riddance."

I remain unobtrusive ... even to myself.

FACE IN THE WELL

Jenny hee-haws "hello" from her stockade
as a burdened donkey friend, happy to be home,
trails the goat herd down a desert slope toward
the village sweet water well and corral.

Copper goat bells signal the day is nearly
done as around the hand-drawn water well
the floppy-eared goats await their shepherd to pour
water they have longed for all the dusty day.

Bleating expectantly, they impatiently await
and nudge the young shepherd to pull the elixir
bucket up from the well, then quickly drink their fill
until thirst sated, heads begin to rise, jaws dripping.

Now gazing vacantly at sky and clouds
while dreaming of oats and cooler night air,
all shuffle away, leaving me sitting alone on the
well's weathered frame looking down at the water.

Sky and clouds are reflected on the water mirror,
and when I lean forward, my head, face and shoulders
are framed by blue sky, rather like an Roman-era depiction
of a bearded deity looking down from clouds in heaven.

The image makes me laugh, especially when
a loose pebble falls into the well, making my gallant
reflection wiggle, then split apart until it slowly
reassembles from galaxy-like spirals.

Punta Prieta Baja California

WE WERE FORGED TO BEND

I think often on our lofty plans,
youthful endeavors,
our serious scholarly ways.
How we debated every new thought
(and every thought was new),
analyzed every thing we saw,
each man we met, the nature of mountains
and plants and insects and birds,
of bigotry and love — all dissected.
I and a few mates, cocked and unafraid,
eased into the Forgotten Peninsula
anxious to taste trial and danger.
Both came often enough,
making us tough-minded
and energized for a lifetime.
Certain in our values and views,
at times too quick to censure
those with whom we differed,
learned the value of tempered words
in a land without law where men
had hard fists and nature was unforgiving.
Frontier people unveiled mettle's value,
respect for men, honesty with nature
... welding prudence onto bravado.
Sobered by beauty, hardship, and pain
we watched eagles take prey,
hiked deserts picked clean by survivors,
shared the elegant simplicity of wilderness people,
listened to untangled views about justice

and benefitted from unselfish deeds.
Who can forget the adventure, poetry, danger
and inspiration found in a desert furnace
where we were forged to bend?

FRIENDSHIP

Unburdened by duty, we found ourselves
beside a vast, remote and tranquil lagoon
entranced by the sweep of its natural austerity.

Across its nursery waters, Mt. Guerrero Negro
rose massive, silent and triumphant
in black-suited sentinel duty.

The sun, not yet high, bathed the calm water
in reflected planes of silver, blue and gold at play –
molten surfaces dancing toward infinity.

Dune-sitting in silence that begets seeing reality
I found contentment in the realization that my
soul is intertwined with friendships.

As it is said that *no man is an island ...*
so were my depths of joy enriched by sharing
nature's peaceful calm with a friend.

Scammons Lagoon Baja California, Mexico circa 1962
Guerrero Negro means Black Warrior

MORE LIKE PREY

My path snakes between cacti,
mesquite trees and low bushes.
Everything summer hot, clean, undisturbed,
some dead plants dried to a crisp.

On a low rise is a stand of sahuaro
soberly conferring on the nature
of the universe and if turtles fly at night.
Farther on, a rough rise covered with
egg-shaped brown boulders, perhaps
twenty feet high amidst wind blown
white sand and gray-green bushes.

A beautiful but formidable tranquility.

Walking around the outcrop, I hope
a valley will unfold beyond, and it does,
but the boulder field lures me back
to wander in its cathedral-like atmosphere.

I find a swale tufted with green grass and
a small pool of clear water."What an ambrosial
find" I whisper while descending into its charm,
but then stop when I spy paw prints of large kitties.
Suddenly I feel more like prey than an explorer.

Arizona

THE FINALITY OF IT

Finally skilled in survival hunting
for the protein that meat provides —-
but hunting begins to haunt.

Killing – the finality of it -
defenseless rabbits, their
eyes always open in death.
Translucent, lifeless black agates
looking back at me in despair,
a well of infinity and irrevocable death!

Soft warm body, limp in my hands.
Head and long ears flop.
Athletic legs stilled forever.
A breeze musses his fluff.

Tethered to death by my bullet,
the ground beneath his perfect bantam
corpse is fouled with blood and intestine
blown out by the violent impact.

My gun now silent in its holster,
I had not seen hunting this way before.

CANDLES

We brought no candles
on our first expedition
but witnessing the soft
warm light wax flame yields
on untroubled nights in homes
of remote rural homesteads ,
we traded for some at first chance.
Candlelight brushes all it touches
with a peaceful golden voice.